THEME AND VARIATIONS

Theme and Variations

A Poetry Anthology

Selected and arranged by R. B. HEATH

Head of the Department of English,
Wellesbourne County Secondary School, High Wycombe

LONGMANS

LONGMANS, GREEN & CO LTD
London and Harlow

*Associated companies, branches and
representatives throughout the world*

© *R. B. Heath* 1965
First published 1965
Third impression 1969

*Printed in Great Britain by
Western Printing Services Limited, Bristol*

Editor's Note

This anthology contains a selection of poetry on a theme suggested by the following quotation from De Tocqueville:

'The destinies of mankind, man himself taken aloof from his country and age, and standing in the presence of Nature and God, with his passions, his doubts, his rare prosperities and inconceivable wretchedness, will become the chief, if not the sole, theme of poetry.'

The selection of poetry has been grouped and arranged in sequence in order to provide a thought-provoking anthology in which the individual poem is seen in relationship to another, and in a common relationship to the main theme.

The book is intended for use in the appreciation of emotional expression, the formulation and extension of ideas, and as a basis for discussion and further reading.

Contents

God and Nature

Man Himself

viii

God and Nature

1 *Master Plan*

Design

I found a dimpled spider, fat and white,
On a white heal-all, holding up a moth
Like a white piece of rigid satin cloth—
Assorted characters of death and blight
Mixed ready to begin the morning right,
Like the ingredients of a witches' broth—
A snow-drop spider, a flower like froth,
And dead wings carried like a paper kite.

What had that flower to do with being white,
The wayside blue and innocent heal-all?
What brought the kindred spider to that height,
Then steered the white moth thither in the night?
What but design of darkness to appal?—
If design govern in a thing so small.

Robert Frost

Four Trees

Four trees upon a solitary acre
Without design
Or order or apparent action
Maintain.

The sun upon a morning meets them,
The wind;
No nearer neighbour have they
But God.

The acre gives them place,
They, him, attention of passer-by—
Of shadow, or of squirrel, haply,
Or boy.

What deed is theirs unto the general nature,
What plan
They severally promote or hinder,
Unknown.

Emily Dickinson

God and Man

Say first, of God above, or Man below,
What can we reason, but from what we know?
Of Man, what see we, but his station here,
From which to reason, or to which refer?
Thro' worlds unnumber'd tho' the God be known,
'Tis ours to trace him only in our own.
He, who thro' vast immensity can pierce,
See worlds on worlds compose one universe,
Observe how system into system runs,
What other planets circle other suns,
What vary'd Being peoples ev'ry star,
May tell why Heav'n has made us as we are.

Alexander Pope
AN ESSAY ON MAN

The Undiscovered Planet

Out on the furthest tether let it run
Its hundred-year-long orbit, cold
As solid mercury, old and dead
Before *this* world's fermenting bread
Had got a crust to cover it; landscape of lead
Whose purple voes and valleys are
Lit faintly by a sun
No nearer than a measurable star.

No man has seen it; nor the lensed eye
That pin-points week by week the same patch of sky
Records even a blur across its pupil; only
The errantry of Saturn, the wry
Retarding of Uranus, speak
Of the pull beyond the pattern: –
The unknown is shown
Only by a bend in the known.

Norman Nicholson

from *Darkness*

I had a dream, which was not all a dream.
The bright sun was extinguish'd, and the stars
Did wander darkling in the eternal space,
Rayless, and pathless, and the icy earth
Swung blind and blackening in the moonless air;
Morn came and went—and came, and brought no day,
And men forgot their passions in the dread
Of this their desolation; and all hearts
Were chilled into a selfish prayer for light . . .
Happy were those who dwelt within the eye
Of the volcanoes, and their mountain-torch:
A fearful hope was all the world contained;
Forests were set on fire—but hour by hour
They fell and faded—and the crackling trunks
Extinguish'd with a crash—and all was black . . .
And War, which for a moment was no more,
Did glut himself again:—a meal was bought
With blood, and each sate sullenly apart
Gorging himself in gloom: no love was left;
All earth was but one thought—and that was death
Immediate and inglorious . . .
                    The world was void,
The populous and the powerful was a lump
Seasonless, herbless, treeless, manless, lifeless—
A lump of death—a chaos of hard clay.
The rivers, lakes, and ocean all stood still,
And nothing stirred within their silent depths;
Ships sailorless lay rotting on the sea,
And their masts fell down piecemeal: as they dropp'd
They slept on the abyss without a surge—

The waves were dead; the tides were in their grave,
The moon, their mistress, had expired before;
The winds were wither'd in the stagnant air,
And the clouds perish'd; Darkness had no need
Of aid from them—She was the Universe.

Lord Byron

Further Reading

ELIZABETH JENNINGS. World I have not made. *Poems for a Birth or a Death*, Deutsch; or *An Anthology of Commonwealth Verse*, Blackie.

CARL SANDBURG. Personality. *Selected Poems*, Cape; or *The Faber Book of Modern American Verse*, Faber.

NORMAN NICHOLSON. The Expanding Universe; The Outer Planet; The Unseen Centre. *The Pot Geranium*, Faber.

LORD BYRON. Darkness. *Poetical Works*, Oxford University Press; or *The Mentor Book of Major British Poets*, The New English Library.

LOUIS MACNEICE. Star-Gazer; Budgie. *The Burning Perch*, Faber.

ALEXANDER POPE. An Essay on Man, Epistle 1. *The Collected Poems of Alexander Pope*, Dent, Everyman's Library; or any standard edition.

2 Chance or Design?

Auto Wreck

Its quick soft silver bell beating, beating,
And down the dark one ruby flare
Pulsing out red light like an artery,
The ambulance at top speed floating down
Past beacons and illuminated clocks
Wings in a heavy curve, dips down,
And breaks speed, entering the crowd.
The doors leap open, emptying light;
Stretchers are laid out, the mangled lifted
And stowed into the little hospital.
Then the bell, breaking the hush, tolls once,
And the ambulance with its terrible cargo
Rocking, slightly rocking, moves away,
As the doors, an afterthought, are closed.
We are deranged, walking among the cops
Who sweep glass and are large and composed.
One is still making notes under the light.
One with a bucket douches ponds of blood
Into the street and gutter.
One hangs on the wrecks that cling,
Empty husks of locusts, to iron poles.

Our throats were tight as tourniquets,
Our feet were bound with splints, but now,
Like convalescents intimate and gauche,
We speak through sickly smiles and warn
With the stubborn saw of commonsense,
The grim joke and the banal resolution.
The traffic moves round with care,
But we remain, touching a wound
That opens to our richest horror.
Already old, the question Who shall die?
Becomes unspoken Who is innocent?
For death in war is done by hands;
Suicide has cause and stillbirth, logic;

And cancer, simple as a flower, blooms.
But this invites the occult mind,
Cancels our physics with a sneer,
And spatters all we knew of denouement.
Across the expedient and wicked stones.

Karl Shapiro

The Convergence of the Twain

(Lines on the loss of the 'Titanic')

In a solitude of the sea
Deep from human vanity,
And the Pride of Life that planned her, stilly couches she.

Steel chambers, late the pyres
Of her salamandrine fires,
Cold currents thrid, and turn to rhythmic tidal lyres.

Over the mirrors meant
To glass the opulent
The sea-worm crawls—grotesque, slimed, dumb, indifferent.

Jewels in joy designed
To ravish the sensuous mind
Lie lightless, all their sparkles bleared and black and blind.

Dim moon-eyed fishes near
Gaze at the gilded gear
And query: 'What does this vaingloriousness down here?'

Well: while was fashioning
This creature of cleaving wing,
The Immanent Will that stirs and urges everything

Prepared a sinister mate
For her—so gaily great—
A Shape of Ice, for the time far and dissociate.

And as the smart ship grew
In stature, grace and hue,
In shadowy silent distance grew the Iceberg too.

Alien they seemed to be:
No mortal eye could see
The intimate welding of their later history.

Or sign that they were bent
By paths coincident
On being anon twin halves of one august event,

Till the Spinner of the Years
Said 'Now!' And each one hears,
And consummation comes, and jars two hemispheres.

Thomas Hardy

from *The Rubaiyat of Omar Khayyam*

'Tis all a Chequer-board of Nights and Days
    Where Destiny with Men for Pieces plays:
  Hither and thither moves, and mates, and slays.
And one by one back in the Closet lays.

The Ball no Question makes of Ayes and Noes,
    But Right or Left as strikes the Player goes;
  And He that toss'd Thee down into the Field,
He knows about it all—HE knows—HE knows!

The Moving Finger writes; and, having writ,
    Moves on; nor all thy Piety nor Wit
  Shall lure it back to cancel half a Line,
Nor all thy Tears wash out a Word of it.

And that inverted Bowl we call The Sky,
    Whereunder crawling coopt we live and die,
  Lift not thy hands to *It* for help—for It
Rolls impotently on as Thou or I.

Edward Fitzgerald

Hospital for Defectives

By your unnumbered charities
A miracle disclose,
Lord of the Images, whose love
The eyelid and the rose
Takes for a language, and today
Tell to me what is said
By these men in a turnip field
And their unleavened bread.

For all things seem to figure out
The stirrings of your heart,
And two men pick the turnips up
And two men pull the cart;
And yet between the four of them
No word is ever said
Because the yeast was not put in
Which makes the human bread.
But three men stare on vacancy
And one man strokes his knees;
What is the meaning to be found
In such dark vowels as these?

Lord of the Images, whose love
The eyelid and the rose
Takes for a metaphor, today
Beneath the warder's blows,
The unleavened man did not cry out
Or turn his face away;
Through such men in a turnip field
What is it that you say?

Thomas Blackburn

from *In Memoriam A.H.H.*

O yet we trust that somehow good
   Will be the final goal of ill,
   To pangs of nature, sins of will,
Defects of doubt, and taints of blood;

That nothing walks with aimless feet;
   That not one life shall be destroyed,
   Or cast as rubbish to the void,
When God hath made the pile complete;

That not a worm is cloven in vain;
   That not a moth with vain desire
   Is shrivelled in a fruitless fire,
Or but subserves another's gain.

Behold we know not anything;
   I can but trust that good shall fall
   At last—far off—at last, to all,
And every winter change to spring.

So runs my dream; but what am I?
   An infant crying in the night;
   An infant crying for the light;
And with no language but a cry.

Alfred, Lord Tennyson

Further Reading

TED HUGHES. The Casualty. *The Hawk in the Rain*, Faber.

GEORGE BARKER. Circular from America. *The View from a Blind I*, Faber.

ROBERT FROST. 'Out, out—'. *Collected Poems*, Cape; or *Robert Frost*, Penguin Poets.

WILLIAM WORDSWORTH. Intimations of Immortality. *Poetical Works*, Oxford University Press; or *The Mentor Book of Major British Poets*.

PETER LEVI, S.J. What if the World were a Horrible Mad Fit. *The Gravel Pond*, Deutsch.

EDWARD FITZGERALD. *The Rubaiyat of Omar Khayyam*, Collins Classics.

CONRAD AIKEN. The Sounding. *Collected Poems*, Oxford University Press; or *The Faber Book of Modern American Verse*.

THOMAS HARDY. Hap. *Collected Poems*, Macmillan; or *The Mentor Book of Major British Poets*.

3 Man and Nature

Transformations

Portion of this yew
Is a man my grandsire knew,
Bosomed here at its foot:
This branch may be his wife,
A ruddy human life
Now turned to a green shoot.

These grasses must be made
Of her who often prayed,
Last century, for repose;
And the fair girl long ago
Whom I often tried to know
May be entering this rose.

So, they are not underground,
But as nerves and veins abound
In the growths of upper air,
And they feel the sun and rain,
And the energy again
That made them what they were!

Thomas Hardy

from *Tintern Abbey*

> For I have learned
> To look on nature, not as in the hour
> Of thoughtless youth; but hearing oftentimes
> The still, sad music of humanity,
> Nor harsh nor grating, though of ample power
> To chasten and subdue. And I have felt
> A presence that disturbs me with the joy
> Of elevated thoughts; a sense sublime
> Of something far more deeply interfused,
> Whose dwelling is the light of setting suns,
> And the round ocean and the living air,
> And the blue sky, and in the mind of man;
> A motion and a spirit, that impels
> All thinking things, all objects of all thought,
> And rolls through all things. Therefore am I still
> A lover of the meadows and the woods,
> And mountains; and of all that we behold
> From this green earth; of all the mighty world
> Of eye, and ear,—both what they half create,
> And what perceive; well pleased to recognise
> In nature and the language of the sense,
> The anchor of my purest thoughts, the nurse,
> The guide, the guardian of my heart, and soul
> Of all my moral being.

William Wordsworth

Salthouse, Norfolk

Even on midsummer days a spongy mist
Swirls round the marshes and the sun is subdued.
The sluggish grey sea's thud and the stark flint church
Emphasize the silence and the solitude.

It may be human fantasy that lends
An aspect of desolation to this village.
We are saddened to reflect that sullen tides,
Lashed from somnolence, will rise and pillage

The hoarded treasure of these fishermen
Who stubbornly breed their pigs and ducks and cows,
Knowing a score of years the longest respite
The whim of Nature contemptuously allows.

Perhaps if we came here with unburdened hearts
The marram grass and salt marsh would assume
The savour and the promise of ripening corn
And the sea would flash with iridescent spume.

But I believe that some original taint
Haunts and infects with foreboding the heavy skies,
Benumbing the flints and beasts and earth with grief
Which we do not invent but recognise.

John Press

To an Independent Preacher

Who preached that we should be 'in harmony with Nature'

'In harmony with Nature'? Restless fool,
Who with such heat dost preach what were to thee,
When true, the last impossibility;
To be like Nature strong, like Nature cool:—
Know, man hath all which Nature hath, but more,
And in that *more* lie all his hopes of good.
Nature is cruel; man is sick of blood:
Nature is stubborn; man would fain adore:
Nature is fickle; man hath need of rest:
Nature forgives no debt, and fears no grave:
Man would be mild, and with safe conscience blest.
Man must begin, know this, where Nature ends;
Nature and man can never be fast friends.
Fool, if thou canst not press her, rest her slave!

Matthew Arnold

Further Reading

WILLIAM WORDSWORTH. Influence of Natural Objects; Lines written in Early Spring; Tintern Abbey. *Poetical Works*, Oxford University Press.

JOHN WAIN. Reason for not writing Orthodox Nature Poetry. *A Word Carved on a Sill*, Routledge.

NORMAN NICHOLSON. The Land under Ice. *Rock Face*, Faber.

LAURIE LEE. Day of These Days. *Bloom of Candles*, Lehmann.

HARRIET PLUMPTON. Thine is the Power. *Out of the North*. Oxford University Press.

JOHN CLARE. Pastoral Poesy. *An Anthology of Commonwealth Verse*, Blackie.

NORMAN NICHOLSON. Thomas Gray in Patterdale. *Rock Face*, Faber.

4 *The Fuse of Time*

Field of Autumn

Slow moves the acid breath of noon
over the copper-coated hill,
slow from the wild crab's bearded breast
the palsied apples fall.

Like coloured smoke the day hangs fire,
taking the village without sound;
the vulture-headed sun lies low
chained to the violet ground.

The horse upon the rocky height
rolls all the valley in his eye,
but dares not raise his foot or move
his shoulder from the fly.

The sheep, snail-backed against the wall,
lifts her blind face but does not know
the cry her blackened tongue gives forth
is the first bleat of snow.

Each bird and stone, each roof and well,
feels the gold foot of autumn pass;
each spider binds with glittering snare
the splintered bones of grass.

Slow moves the hour that sucks our life,
slow drops the late wasp from the pear,
the rose tree's thread of scent draws thin—
and snaps upon the air.

Laurie Lee

Koré

Yea, she hath passed hereby and blessed the sheaves
And the great garths and stacks and quiet farms,
And all the tawny and the crimson leaves,
Yea, she hath passed with poppies in her arms
Under the star of dusk through stealing mist
And blest the earth and gone while no man wist.

With slow reluctant feet and weary eyes
And eyelids heavy with the coming sleep,
With small breasts lifted up in stress of sighs,
She passed as shadows pass amid the sheep
While the earth dreamed and only I was 'ware
Of that faint fragrance blown from her soft hair.

The land lay steeped in peace of silent dreams,
There was no sound amid the sacred boughs
Nor any mournful music in her streams,
Only I saw the shadow on her brows,
Only I knew her for the Yearly Slain
And wept, and weep until she come again.

Frederic Manning

The force that through the green fuse drives the flower

The force that through the green fuse drives the flower
Drives my green age; that blasts the roots of trees
Is my destroyer.
And I am dumb to tell the crooked rose
My youth is bent by the same wintry fever.

The force that drives the water through the rocks
Drives my red blood; that dries the mouthing streams
Turns mine to wax.
And I am dumb to mouth unto my veins
How at the mountain spring the same mouth sucks

The hand that whirls the water in the pool
Stirs the quicksand; that ropes the blowing wind
Hauls my shroud sail.
And I am dumb to tell the hanging man
How of my clay is made the hangman's lime.

The lips of time leech to the fountain head;
Love drips and gathers, but the fallen blood
Shall calm her sores.
And I am dumb to tell a weather's wind
How time has ticked a heaven round the stars.

And I am dumb to tell the lover's tomb
How at my sheet goes the same crooked worm.

Dylan Thomas

November

The month of the drowned dog. After long rain the land
Was black, sodden as the bed of an ancient lake;
Treed with iron and birdless. I took the sunk lane
Where the ditch—a seep silent all summer—

Made brown foam with a big voice; that, and my boots
On the lane's scrubbed stones, in the gulleyed leaves,
Against the hill's hanging silence;
Mist silvering the droplets on the bare thorns

Slower than the change of daylight.
In a let of the ditch a tramp was bundled asleep,
Face tucked down into beard, drawn in
Under its hair like a hedgehog's. I took him for dead,

But his stillness separated from the death
Of the rotting grass and the ground as a wind chilled,
And a new comfort tightened through him;
Each hand stuffed deeper into the other sleeve;

His ankles, bound with sacking and hairy band,
Rubbed each other, resettling. The wind chilled,
And a puff shook a glittering from the thorns.
Again the rains' dragging grey columns

Smudged the farms, and in a moment
The fields were jumping and smoking; the thorns
Quivered, riddled with the glassy verticals.
I stayed on under the welding cold

Watching the tramp's face glisten and the drops on his coat
Flash and darken. I thought what strong trust
Slept in him—as the trickling furrows slept,
And the thorn-roots in their grip on darkness;

And the buried stones, taking the weight of winter;
The hill where the hare crouched with clenched teeth.
Rain plastered the land till it was shining
Like hammered lead, and I ran, and in the rushing wood

Under a dark sheltering oak leaned.
The keeper's gibbet had owls and hawks
By the neck, weasels, a gang of cats, crows;
Some, stiff, weightless, twirled like dry bark bits

In the drilling rain. But some still had their shape,
Had their pride with it; hung, chins on chests,
Patient to outwait these worst days that beat
Their crowns bare and dripped from their feet.

Ted Hughes

Further Reading

DYLAN THOMAS. Especially When the October Wind. *Collected Poems*, Dent; or *The Mentor Book of Major British Poets*.

W. H. AUDEN. The Hour-Glass Whispers to the Lion's Paw. *Another Time, Nones*. Faber; *An Anthology of Modern Verse 1940–1960*, Methuen.

PHILIP LARKIN. Triple Time. *The Less Deceived*, Marvell, or *An Anthology of Modern Verse 1940–1960*.

ROBERT FROST. My November Guest. *The Complete Works of Robert Frost*, Cape; or *Robert Frost*, Penguin Poets.

ALEXANDER BAIRD. Fire in November. *Poems*, Chatto and Windus.

KEITH DOUGLAS. Time Eating. *Collected Poems*, Editions Poetry London, or *The Faber Book of Modern Verse*.

PATRICK KAVANAGH. October. *Come Dance with Kitty Stobling*, Longmans; or *45–60: An Anthology of English Poetry 1945–60*, Putnam.

ARCHIBALD MACLEISH. Signature for Tempo. *Collected Poems*, Houghton Mifflin; or *Modern Verse in English 1900–50*, Eyre and Spottiswoode.

ROBERT GRAVES. Time. *Collected Poems*, Cassell; or *The Faber Book of Modern Verse*.

5 Nature in Control

Storm Fear

When the wind works against us in the dark,
And pelts with snow
The lower chamber window on the east,
And whispers with a sort of stifled bark,
The beast,
'Come out! Come out!'—
It costs no inward struggle not to go,
Ah, no!
I count our strength,
Two and a child,
Those of us not asleep subdued to mark
How the cold creeps as the fire dies at length,—
How drifts are piled,
Dooryard and road ungraded,
Till even the comforting barn grows far away,
And my heart owns a doubt
Whether 'tis in us to arise with day
And save ourselves unaided.

Robert Frost

Drought

Heat, all-pervading, crinkles up the soil;
A deathly silence numbs the molten air;
On beds of rivers, islands scorched and bare,
Warm scavengers of wind heap up the spoil;
And wide-eyed oxen, gaunt and spent with toil,
Huddled together near some shrunken pool—
Pant for the shade of trees and pastures cool,
Lashing their tails at flies they cannot foil.
Whilst overhead, the sun-god drives his way
Through halting hours of blinding, blazing, light,
Until his shining steeds a moment stay
And disappear behind the gates of night.
And still no rain. A cloudless, starlit sky
Watches the veld, and all things droop and die.

Denys Lefebvre

Cloud-Burst

The clouds are beaten silver plaques
Hollowed, with gleaming joins,
Until the madman storm attacks
And the wild lightning foins;

The whole sky, loosened like ripped foil,
Crackles about the privets,
And the rain bounces on the soil
In showers of silver rivets.

On the one house in all the fen
Why should their malice settle?
Furious upon it, again, again,
Drops crepitating metal.

Burst of long-gathering destinies
On the bald head of Lear?
Not here such royal doom there is,
Not Oedipus is here,

And yet the same high kingly sorrow,
An old man, too, and lonely:
He sees the flood-banks burst, the morrow
Blind desolation only.

He is not crying for his daughters,
But for childhood's fields he ploughed
From youth to strenuous age; the waters
Rush on him, broken, bowed.

Geoffrey Johnson

Hunger

I come among the peoples like a shadow.
I sit down by each man's side.

None sees me, but they look on one another,
And know that I am there.

My silence is like the silence of the tide
That buries the playground of children;

Like the deepening of frost in the slow night,
When birds are dead in the morning.

Armies trample, invade, destroy,
With guns roaring from earth and air.

I am more terrible than armies,
I am more feared than cannon.

Kings and chancellors give commands;
I give no command to any;

But I am listened to more than kings
And more than passionate orators.

I unswear words, and undo deeds.
Naked things know me.

I am the first and last to be felt of the living.
I am Hunger.

Laurence Binyon

Our Hold on the Planet

We asked for rain. It didn't flash and roar.
It didn't lose its temper at our demand
And blow a gale. It didn't misunderstand
And give us more than our spokesman bargained for;
And just because we owned to a wish for rain,
Send us a flood and bid us be damned and drown.
It gently threw us a glittering shower down.
And when we had taken that into the roots of grain,
It threw us another and then another still
Till the spongy soil again was natal wet.
We may doubt the just proportion of good to ill.
There is much in nature against us. But we forget:
Take nature altogether since time began,
Including human nature, in peace and war,
And it must be a little more in favour of man,
Say a fraction of one per cent at the very least,
Or our number living wouldn't be steadily more,
Our hold on the planet wouldn't have so increased.

Robert Frost

Further Reading

TED HUGHES. Wind. *The Hawk in the Rain*; or *The New Poetry*, Penguin.

MICHAEL BALDWIN. Storm; Floods are not the Flood. *Death on a Live Wire*, Longmans.

FRANCIS CAREY SLATER. Drought. *An Anthology of Commonwealth Verse*, Blackie.

GEOFFREY JOHNSON. Drought. *The Ninth Wave*, Harrap.

TRISTRAM COFFIN. The Fog. *Collected Poems*, Macmillan; or *The Faber Book of Modern American Verse*.

D. H. LAWRENCE. Storm in the Black Forest. *Collected Poems*, Heinemann.

CHRISTOPHER MIDDLETON. The Thousand Things. *Torse 3*, Longmans.

6 War Against Nature

Slate

Behind the higher hill
sky slides away to fringe of crumbling cloud;
out of the gorse-grown slope
the quarry bites its tessellated tiers.

The rain-eroded slate packs loose and flat
in broken sheets and frigid swathes of stone,
like withered petals of a great grey flower.

The quarry is deserted now; within
a scooped-out niche of rubble, dust and silt
a single slate-roofed hut to ruin falls.

A petrified chaos
the quarry is; the slate makes still-born waves,
or crumbling clouds like those
behind the hill, monotonously grey.

David Gascoyne

The War against the Trees

The man who sold his lawn to Standard Oil
Joked with his neighbours come to watch the show
While the bulldozers, drunk with gasoline,
Tested the virtue of the soil
Under the branchy sky
By overthrowing first the privet-row.

Forsythia-forays and hydrangea-raids
Were but preliminaries to a war
Against the great-grandfathers of the town,
So freshly lopped and maimed.
They struck and struck again,
And with each elm a century went down.

All day the hireling engines charged the trees,
Subverting them by hacking underground
In grub-dominions, where dark summer's mole
Rampages through his halls,
Till a northern seizure shook
Those crowns, forcing the giants to their knees.

I saw the ghosts of children at their games
Racing beyond their childhood in the shade,
And while the green world turned its death-foxed page
And a red wagon wheeled,
I watch them disappear
Into the suburbs of their grievous age.

Ripped from the craters much too big for hearts
The club-roots bared their amputated coils,
Raw gorgons matted blind, whose pocks and scars
Cried Moon! on a corner lot
One witness-moment, caught
In the rear-view mirrors of the passing cars.

Stanley Kunitz
48

The Jaguar

The apes yawn and adore their fleas in the sun.
The parrots shriek as if they were on fire, or strut
Like cheap tarts to attract the stroller with the nut.
Fatigued with indolence, tiger and lion

Lie still as the sun. The boa-constrictor's coil
Is a fossil. Cage after cage seems empty, or
Stinks of sleepers from the breathing straw.
It might be painted on the nursery wall.

But who runs like the rest past these arrives
At a cage where the crowd stands, stares, mesmerized,
As a child at a dream, at a jaguar hurrying enraged
Through prison darkness after the drills of his eyes

On a short fierce fuse. Not in boredom—
The eye satisfied to be blind in fire,
By the bang of blood in the brain deaf the ear—
He spins from the bars, but there's no cage to him

More than the visionary his cell:
His stride is wildernesses of freedom:
The world rolls under the long thrust of his heel.
Over the cage floor the horizons come.

Ted Hughes

The Sabbath

Waking on the Seventh Day of Creation,
  They cautiously sniffed the air:
The most fastidious nostril among them admitted
  That fellow was no longer there.

Herbivore, parasite, predator scouted,
  Migrants flew fast and far—
Not a trace of his presence: holes in the earth,
  Beaches covered with tar.

Ruins and metallic rubbish in plenty
  Were all that was left of him
Whose birth on the Sixth had made of that day
  An unnecessary interim.

Well, that fellow had never really smelled
  Like a creature who would survive:
No grace, address or faculty like those
  Born on the First Five.

Back, then, at last on a natural economy,
  Now His Impudence was gone,
Looking exactly like what it was,
  The Seventh Day went on,

Beautiful, happy, perfectly pointless . . .
  A rifle's ringing crack
Split their Arcadia wide open, cut
  Their Sabbath nonsense short.

For whom did they think they had been created?
  That fellow was back,
More bloody-minded than they remembered,
  More god-like than they thought.

W. H. Auden

Further Reading

LOUIS MACNEICE. The Pet Shop. *The Burning Perch*, Faber.

CHRISTOPHER MIDDLETON. The Greenfly. *Torse 3*, Longmans.

NORMAN NICHOLSON. Millom Old Quarry. *The Pot Geranium*, Faber; or *The Harrap Book of Modern Verse*, Harrap.

F. L. LUCAS. Beleaguered Cities. *From Many Times and Lands*, John Lane; or *Poems of Our Time*, Dent, Everyman's Library.

STANLEY SNAITH. To Some Builders of Cities. *The Harrap Book of Modern Verse*.

HERBERT PALMER. The Wounded Hawk. *Collected Poems*, Hart-Davis.

GERARD MANLEY HOPKINS. Binsey Poplars. *The Complete Book of Poems*, Oxford University Press; or *Flash Point*, E. J. Arnold.

RUTH PITTER. The Tigress. *Urania*, Cresset Press.

ROBERT GRAVES. In the Wilderness. *An Anthology of Modern Verse*, Methuen.

GORDON BOTTOMLEY. To Iron-Founders and Others. *An Anthology of Modern Verse*, Methuen.

7 The Inheritors

Mushrooms

Overnight, very
Whitely, discreetly,
Very quietly
Our toes, our noses
Take hold on the loam,
Acquire the air.

Nobody sees us,
Stops us, betrays us;
The small grains make room.

Soft fists insist on
Heaving the needles,
The leafy bedding,

Even the paving,
Our hammers, our rams,
Earless and eyeless,

Perfectly voiceless,
Widen the crannies,
Shoulder through holes. We

Diet on water,
On crumbs of shadow,
Bland-mannered, asking

Little or nothing.
So many of us!
So many of us!

We are shelves, we are
Tables, we are meek,
We are edible,

Nudgers and shovers
In spite of ourselves.
Our kind multiplies:

We shall by morning
Inherit the earth.
Our foot's in the door.

Sylvia Plath

Thistles

Against the rubber tongues of cows and the hoeing hands of men
Thistles spike the summer air
And crackle open under a blue-black pressure.

Every one a revengeful burst
Of resurrection, a grasped fistful
Of splintered weapons and Icelandic frost thrust up

From the underground stain of a decayed Viking.
They are like pale hair and the gutturals of dialects.
Every one manages a plume of blood.

Then they grow grey like men
Mown down, it is a feud. Their sons appear
Stiff with weapons, fighting back over the same ground.

Ted Hughes

The Last Chrysanthemum

Why should this flower delay so long
    To show its tremulous plumes?
Now is the time of plaintive robin-song,
    When flowers are in their tombs.

Through the slow summer, when the sun
    Called to each frond and whorl
That all he could for flowers was being done,
    Why did it not uncurl?

It must have felt that fervid call
    Although it took no heed,
Waking but now, when leaves like corpses fall,
    And saps all retrocede.

Too late its beauty, lonely thing,
    The season's shine is spent,
Nothing remains for it but shivering
    In tempests turbulent.

Had it a reason for delay,
    Dreaming in witlessness
That for a bloom so delicately gay
    Winter would stay its stress?

—I talk as if the thing were born
    With sense to work its mind;
Yet it is but one mask of many worn
    By the Great Face behind.

Thomas Hardy

A Daisy

Look unoriginal
Being numerous. They ask for attention
With that gradated yellow swelling
Of oily stamens. Petals focus them:
The eye-lashes grow wide.
Why should not one bring these to a funeral?
And at night, like children,
Without anxiety, their consciousness
Shut with white petals.

Blithe, individual.

The unwearying, small sunflower
Fills the grass
With versions of one eye.
A strength in the full look
Candid, solid, glad.
Domestic as milk.

In multitudes, wait,
Each, to be looked at, spoken to.
They do not wither;
Their going, a pressure
Of elate sympathy
Released from you.
Rich up to the last interval
With minute tubes of oil, pollen;
Utterly without scent, for the eye,
For the eye, simply. For the mind
And its invisible organ,
That feeling thing.

Jon Silkin

Further Reading

LAURIE LEE. Thistle. *Bloom of Candles*, Lehmann.

D. H. LAWRENCE. Sicilian Cyclamens; Bavarian Gentians. *Collected Poems of D. H. Lawrence*, Heinemann; or *D. H. Lawrence*, Penguin Poets.

LOTTE ZURNDORFER. Peony. *Poems*, Hogarth; or *An Anthology of Modern Verse 1940–1960*, Methuen.

ALLEN GINSBERG. In back of the real. *Howl*, City Lights Books; or *Beat Poets*, Vista Books, Pocket Poets.

MURIEL STUART. The Seed Shop. *Poems*, Heinemann; or *Poems of Our Time, 1900–1960*, Dent.

CHRISTOPHER MIDDLETON. Rhododendron Estranged in Twilight. *Torse 3*, Longmans.

E. J. SCOVELL. Shadows of Chrysanthemums. *Shadows of Chrysanthemums*, Routledge; or *Modern Verse in English 1900–50*, Eyre and Spottiswoode.

RICHARD WILBUR. Potato. *Poems, 1943–1956*, Faber; or *The Faber Book of Modern American Verse*.

WILLIAM BLAKE. The Sick Rose. *The Mentor Book of Major British Poets*.

TED HUGHES. Snowdrop. *The Hawk in the Rain*, Faber; or *The New Poetry*, Penguin.

8 Man with Animals

Laggandoan, Harris

Bullock bellied in a green marsh,
Chinning his blockhead among white
And yellow tiny flowers, rolls
His brown eyes in a dark delight.

A dragon-fly of mica whirs
Off and up; then makes a thin
Tottering grass its anchor-post,
Changed to a small blue zeppelin.

And Joseph-coated frogs tumble
Like drunken heralds in the grass
That tipples sweet marsh water and
Defies the sun's broad burning-glass.

Down from the moor, between two rocks
The furnace sun has calcined white,
Johann, humped with a creel of peats,
Comes leaning forward through the light.

Then everything returns again
To timelessness. A grasshopper scours
His little pail; and blissfully
The bullock floats awash in flowers.

Norman MacCaig

The Zebras

From the dark woods that breathe of fallen showers,
Harnessed with level rays in golden reins,
The zebras draw the dawn across the plains
Wading knee-deep among the scarlet flowers.
The sunlight, zithering their flanks with fire,
Flashes between the shadows as they pass
Barred with electric tremors through the grass
Like wind along the gold strings of a lyre.

Into the flushed air snorting rosy plumes
That smoulder round their feet in drifting fumes,
With dove-like voices call the distant fillies,
While round the herds the stallion wheels his flight,
Engine of beauty volted with delight,
To roll his mare among the trampled lilies.

Roy Campbell

Mallard

Squawking they rise from reeds into the sun,
climbing like furies, running on blood and bone,
with wings like garden shears clipping the misty air,
four mallard, hard-winged, with necks like rods
fly in perfect over the marsh.

Keeping their distance, gyring, not letting slip the air,
but leaping into it straight like hounds or divers,
they stretch out into the wind and sound their horns again.

Suddenly siding to bank of air unbidden
by hand signal or morse message of command
downsky they plane, sliding like corks on a current,
designed so deftly that all air is advantage,

till, with few flaps, orderly as they left the earth,
alighting among curlew they pad on mud.

Rex Warner

Me and the Animals

I share my kneebones with the gnat,
My joints with ferrets, eyes with rat
Or blind bat, blinking owl, the goat
His golden cloven orb. I mate like a stoat,
Or like the heavy whale, that moves a sea
To make a mother's gross fecundity.

I share lung's action with the snake;
The fish is cold, but vertebrate like me; my steak
Is muscle from a butcher's arm, a butcher's heart
Is some sheep's breast that throbbed; I start
At noise with ears which in a dog
Can hear what I cannot; in water I'm a frog.

I differ most in lacking their content
To be, no more. They're at mercy of the scent,
Of hot, cold, summer, winter, hunger, anger,
Or ritual establishing the herd, smelling out the stranger:
I walk upright, alone, ungoverned, free:
Yet their occasional lust, fear, unease, walk with me
Always. All ways.

David Holbrook

The Images of Death

The hawk, the furred eagle, the smooth panther—
Images of desire and power, images of death,
These we adore and fear, these we need,
Move in the solitude of night or the tall sky,
Move with a strict grace to the one fulfilment:
The Greenland falcon, the beautiful one,
Lives on carrion and dives inevitably to the prey.

To be human is more difficult:
To be human is to know oneself, to hold the broken mirror,
To become aware of justice, truth, mercy,
To choose the difficult road, to aim
Crookedly, for the direct aim is failure,
To abandon the way of the hawk and the grey falcon.

These fall, and fall stupidly:
To be human is to fall, but not stupidly;
To suffer, but not for a simple end;
To choose, and know the penalty of choice;
To read the intensity of human eyes and features;
To know the intricacy of life and the value of death;
To remember the furred eagle and the smooth panther,
The images of death, and death's simplicity.

Michael Roberts

Further Reading

EDWIN MUIR. The Animals. *Collected Poems*, Faber; or *Flash Point*, E. J. Arnold.

MICHAEL BALDWIN. Man with Animals. *Death on a Live Wire*, Longmans.

W. B. YEATS. Death. *Collected Poems*, Macmillan; or *The English Association Book of Verse*, Allen and Unwin.

TED HUGHES. Hawk Roosting. *Hawk in the Rain*, Faber; or *The New Poetry*, Penguin.

ROBERT HORAN. Little City. *A Beginning*, Yale; or *The Faber Book of Modern American Verse*.

BABETTE DEUTSCH. Young Gazelle. *Anthology of Modern Poetry*, Hutchinson.

RICHARD WILBUR. The Death of a Toad. *Ceremony*, Harcourt Brace; or *Modern Verse in English, 1900–50*, Eyre and Spottiswoode.

RANDALL JARRELL. The Breath of Night. *Selected Poems*, Faber; or *The Faber Book of Modern American Verse*, Faber.

D. H. LAWRENCE. Humming-bird. *Collected Poems*, Heinemann; or *The Mentor Book of Major British Poets*.

Man Himself

9 Responsibilities

The Image

A spider in the bath. The image noted:
Significant maybe but surely cryptic.
A creature motionless and rather bloated,
The barriers shining, vertical and white:
Passing concern, and pity mixed with spite.

Next day with some surprise one finds it there.
It seems to have moved an inch or two, perhaps.
It starts to take on that familiar air
Of prisoners for whom time is erratic:
The filthy aunt forgotten in the attic.

Quite obviously it came up through the waste,
Rejects through ignorance or apathy
That passage back. The problem must be faced;
And life go on though strange intruders stir
Among its ordinary furniture.

One jibs at murder, so a sheet of paper
Is slipped beneath the accommodating legs.
The bathroom window shows for the escaper
The lighted lanterns of laburnum hung
In copper beeches—on which scene it's flung.

We certainly would like thus easily
To cast out of the house all suffering things.
But sadness and responsibility
For our own kind lives in the image noted:
A half-loved creature, motionless and bloated.

Roy Fuller

Old Woman

And she, being old, fed from a mashed plate
as an old mare might droop across a fence
to the dull pastures of its ignorance.
Her husband held her upright while he prayed

to God who is all-forgiving to send down
some angel somewhere who might land perhaps
in his foreign wings among the gradual crops.
She munched, half dead, blindly searching the spoon.

Outside, the grass was raging. There I sat
imprisoned in my pity and my shame
that men and women having suffered time
should sit in such a place, in such a state

and wished to be away, yes, to be far away
with athletes, heroes, Greeks or Roman men
who pushed their bitter spears into a vein
and would not spend an hour with such decay.

'Pray God,' he said, 'we ask you, God,' he said.
The bowed back was quiet. I saw the teeth
tighten their grip around a delicate death.
And nothing moved within the knotted head

but only a few poor veins as one might see
vague wishless seaweed floating on a tide
of all the salty waters where had died
too many waves to mark two more or three.

Iain Crichton Smith

Discord in Childhood

Outside the house an ash-tree hung its terrible whips,
And at night when the wind rose, the lash of the tree
Shrieked and slashed the wind, as a ship's
Weird rigging in a storm shrieks hideously.

Within the house two voices arose, a slender lash
Whistling she-delirious rage, and the dreadful sound
Of a male thong booming and bruising, until it had drowned
The other voice in a silence of blood, 'neath the noise of the ash.

D. H. Lawrence

Incendiary

That one small boy with a face like pallid cheese
And burnt-out little eyes could make a blaze
As brazen, fierce and huge, as red and gold
And zany yellow as the one that spoiled
Three thousand guineas' worth of property
And crops at Godwin's Farm on Saturday
Is frightening, as fact and metaphor:
An ordinary match intended for
The lighting of a pipe or kitchen fire
Misused may set a whole menagerie
Of flame-fanged tigers roaring hungrily.
And frightening, too, that one small boy should set
The sky on fire and choke the stars to heat
Such skinny limbs and such a little heart
Which would have been content with one warm kiss,
Had there been anyone to offer this.

Vernon Scannell

Suicides

Reading the evening papers we meet them,
Those anonymous names:
She who turned the gas on her sorrow,
He whom the Thames
Left one night more derelict on its shore
Than a child at the convent door.

Little we knew them, these who in their lives
Commanded no column.
And even now only between the lines
May we glimpse the solemn
Dilemmas that drove them thither and guess
Something of their last loneliness.

What of this girl? Surely her beauty might
Have confounded the shades?
Or was it beauty itself that led her
Into the glades
Of darkness where, by love's fever oppressed,
She sought to be dispossessed?

And what of him they found in the chilly dawn
With the tide in his hair?
They say in a drowning a man unravels all
His history there
In a fleeting moment before he falls away
On eternal silence. So he may

Have found at last in some long-sought, half-forgotten
Memory a mirror
Reflecting his first true self, distorted since
By childhood terror.
Oh then perhaps—the pattern revealed—too late
He saw his meaningless fate. . . .

We cannot know; for even the notes they left
In their desolate rooms
Can tell us little but that our restless souls
To unknown dooms
Move on—while still, deep in each human face,
We seek the signature of grace.

Tragic their deaths, more tragic the aching thought
That had we been there
We might have laid our hands on their hands and cried
'Do not despair!
For here, even here in this living touch, this breath,
May be the secret you seek in death.'

J. C. Hall

I Sit and Look Out

I sit and look out upon all the sorrows of the world, and upon all
   oppression and shame,
I hear secret convulsive sobs from young men at anguish with
   themselves, remorseful after deeds done,
I see in low life the mother misused by her children, dying,
   neglected, gaunt, desperate,
I see the wife misused by her husband, I see the treacherous
   seducer of young women,
I mark the ranklings of jealousy and unrequited love attempted to
   be hid, I see these sights on earth,
I see the workings of battle, pestilence, tyranny, I see martyrs and
   prisoners,
I observe a famine at sea, I observe the sailors casting lots who
   shall be killed to preserve the lives of the rest,
I observe the slights and degradations cast by arrogant persons
   upon labourers, the poor, and upon negroes, and the like;
All these—all the meanness and agony without end I sitting look
   out upon,
See, hear, and am silent.

Walt Whitman

Further Reading

CHRISTOPHER HAMPTON. Home for Incurables; The Man with the Club-foot. *A Group Anthology*, Oxford University Press.

JOHN BETJEMAN. On a Portrait of a Deaf Man. *Collected Poems*, Murray.

THOMAS BLACKBURN. Felo de Se; An Aftermath. *A Smell of Burning*, Putnam.

ALEXANDER BAIRD. Inmates out for an Airing. *Poems*, Chatto and Windus.

WILFRED OWEN. Maundy Thursday. *The Collected Poems of Wilfred Owen*, Chatto and Windus.

DAVID WRIGHT. Monologue of a Deaf Man. *Monologue of a Deaf Man*, Deutsch; or *45–60: An Anthology of English Poetry 1945–60*, Putnam.

JOHN PUDNEY. This Malefactor. *Collected Poems*, Putnam.

MICHAEL BALDWIN. On Stepping from a Sixth Storey Window. *Death on a Live Wire*, Longmans.

PHILIP LARKIN. No Road. *The Less Deceived*. Marvell Press.

10 *Intolerance*

'Eli, Eli, Lama Sabachthani?'

His breath came in threads, his words were not his own.
He was dying now.
The sun refused to look, and the sky
Closed up its eye. Only the windows of his wounds
Were wide open, and the red curtains of blood
Blew out into the storm, torn to ribbons.
He could no longer fend death off.
Slow, slow, loath to go, hope holds up its head,
Though feet are so sawn through, as a sawn tree that stands
Long, then with one blinding run and blundering tear
Of last despair, scattering its brains and branches on the air,
Slumps, lumps, pitches headlong and thuds, a log clodded clean.
So his last cry and acquiescence. And the vast wall
Of people drew back in awe before that dying fall.
God was dead.

W. R. Rodgers

The Martyrdom of Bishop Farrar

Burned by Bloody Mary's men at Carmarthen. '*If I flinch from the pain of burning, believe not the doctrine that I have preached.*' (*His words on being chained to the stake.*)

Bloody Mary's venomous flames can curl;
They can shrivel sinew and char bone
Of foot, ankle, knee, and thigh, and boil
Bowels, and drop his heart a cinder down;
And her soldiers can cry, as they hurl
Logs in the red rush: 'This is her sermon.'

The sullen-jowled watching Welsh townspeople
Hear him crack in the fire's mouth; they see what
Black oozing twist of stuff bubbles the smell
That tars and retches their lungs: no pulpit
Of his ever held their eyes so still,
Never, as now his agony, his wit.

An ignorant means to establish ownership
Of his flock! Thus their shepherd she seized
And knotted him into this blazing shape
In their eyes, as if such could have cauterized
The trust they turned towards him, and branded on
Its stump her claim, to outlaw question.

So it might have been: seeing their exemplar
And teacher burned for his lessons to black bits,
Their silence might have disowned him to her,
And hung up what he had taught with their Welsh hats:
Who sees his blasphemous father struck by fire
From heaven, might well be heard to speak no oaths.

But the fire that struck here, come from Hell even,
Kindled little heavens in his words
As he fed his body to the flame alive.

Words which, before they will be dumbly spared,
Will burn their body and be tongued with fire
Make paltry folly of flesh and this world's air.

When they saw what annuities of hours
And comfortable blood he burned to get
His words a bare honouring in their ears,
The shrewd townsfolk pocketed them hot;
Stamp was not current but they rang and shone
As good gold as any queen's crown.

Gave all he had, and yet the bargain struck
To a merest farthing his whole agony,
His body's cold-kept miserdom of shrieks
He gave uncounted, while out of his eyes,
Out of his mouth, fire like a glory broke,
And smoke burned his sermons into the skies.

Ted Hughes

Red Balloon

It sailed across the startled town,
over chapels, over chimney pots,
wind-blown above a block of flats
before it floated down.

Oddly, it landed where I stood,
and finding's keeping, as you know.
I breathed on it, I polished it,
till it shone like living blood.

It was my shame, it was my joy,
it brought me notoriety.
From all of Wales the rude boys came,
it ceased to be a toy.

I heard the girls of Cardiff sigh
when my balloon, my red balloon,
soared higher like a happiness
towards the dark blue sky.

Nine months since, I have boasted of
my unique, my only precious;
but to no one dare I show it now
however long they swear their love.

'It's a Jew's balloon,' my best friend cried,
'stained with our dear Lord's blood.'
'That I'm a Jew is true,' I said,
said I, 'that cannot be denied.'

'What relevance?' I asked surprised,
'what's religion to do with this?'
'Your red balloon's a Jew's balloon,
let's get it circumcised.'

Then some boys laughed and some boys cursed,
some unsheathed their dirty knives:
some lunged, some clawed at my balloon,
but still it would not burst.

They bled my nose, they cut my eye,
half conscious in the street I heard,
'Give up, give up your red balloon,'
I don't know exactly why.

Father, bolt the door, turn the key,
lest those sad, brash boys return
to insult my faith and steal
my red balloon from me.

Dannie Abse

Refugee Blues

Say this city has ten million souls,
Some are living in mansions, some are living in holes:
Yet there's no place for us, my dear, yet there's no place for us

Once we had a country and we thought it fair,
Look in the atlas and you'll find it there:
We cannot go there now, my dear, we cannot go there now.

In the village churchyard there grows an old yew,
Every spring it blossoms anew:
Old passports can't do that, my dear, old passports can't do that.

Went to a committee; they offered me a chair;
Asked me politely to return next year:
But where shall we go today, my dear, but where shall we go
    today?

Came to a public meeting; the speaker got up and said:
'If we let them in, they will steal our daily bread';
He was talking of you and me, my dear, he was talking of you
    and me.

.   .   .

Went down to the harbour and stood upon the quay,
Saw the fish swimming as if they were free:
Only ten feet away, my dear, only ten feet away.

Walked through a wood, saw the birds in the trees;
They had no politicians and sang at their ease:
They weren't the human race, my dear, they weren't the human
    race.

Dreamed I saw a building with a thousand floors,
A thousand windows and a thousand doors;
Not one of them was ours, my dear, not one of them was ours.

Stood on a great plain in the falling snow;
Ten thousand soldiers marched to and fro:
Looking for you and me, my dear, looking for you and me.

W. H. Auden

Deep down the blackman's mind

Deep down the blackman's mind there's nothing new
Or bright, save midnight darkness and despair;
We tell you this, we are the ones who dare,
For we have learnt the magic spells that few

Have heard or known. There's horror stacked for you
Behind the blackman's mind. The brain that's there
The cruel homicidal sun flays bone bare,
Then chars the simple dreg an ashen hue.

Oh! if ours be the calm before the storm,
Then this dark sullen cloud may break with sun.
But not in our days. No, not in our days!
No mortal wit may change his shape or form,
Or make the blackman's thoughtless life of fun
Fit him to breed aught but a servile race.

R. E. G. Armattoe

Further Reading

HART CRANE. Black Tambourine. *Collected Poems*, Liveright; or *Oxford Book of American Verse*, Oxford University Press.

KARL SHAPIRO. Nigger. *Collected Poems*, Random House; or *Oxford Book of American Verse*.

WILLIAM SHAKESPEARE. I am a Jew! Hath not a Jew eyes? *The Merchant of Venice*, Act III, Scene 1.

JOHN MILTON. On the Late Massacre in Piedmont, *Palgrave's Golden Treasury*.

MARTIN SEYMOUR-SMITH. The Victims. *Tea with Miss Stockport*, Abelard-Schuman.

ANTHONY THWAITE. In Violent Dreams. *45–60: An Anthology of English Poetry 1945–60*, Putnam.

STEPHEN SPENDER. Memento. *Collected Poems*, Faber; or *Flash Point*, E. J. Arnold.

LORD BYRON. Sonnet on Chillon. *Poetical Works of Lord Byron*, Oxford University Press; or *The Mentor Book of Major British Poets*.

GEORGE MACBETH. The Disciple. *A Group Anthology*, Oxford University Press.

II War

Bayonet Charge

Suddenly he awoke and was running—raw
In raw-seamed hot khaki, his sweat heavy,
Stumbling across a field of clods towards a green hedge
That dazzled with rifle fire, hearing
Bullets smacking the belly out of the air—
He lugged a rifle numb as a smashed arm;
The patriotic tear that had brimmed in his eye
Sweating like molten iron from the centre of his chest,—

In bewilderment then he almost stopped—
In what cold clockwork of the stars and the nations
Was he the hand pointing that second? He was running
Like a man who has jumped up in the dark and runs
Listening between his footfalls for the reason
Of his still running, and his foot hung like
Statuary in mid-stride. Then the shot-slashed furrows

Threw up a yellow hare that rolled like a flame
And crawled in a threshing circle, its mouth wide
Open silent, its eyes standing out.
He plunged past with his bayonet toward the green hedge.
King, honour, human dignity, etcetera
Dropped like luxuries in a yelling alarm
To get out of that blue crackling air
His terror's touchy dynamite.

Ted Hughes

Dulce et Decorum Est

Bent double, like old beggars under sacks,
Knock-kneed, coughing like hags, we cursed through sludge,
Till on the haunting flares we turned our backs,
And towards our distant rest began to trudge.
Men marched asleep. Many had lost their boots,
But limped on, blood-shod. All went lame, all blind;
Drunk with fatigue; deaf even to the hoots
Of gas-shells dropping softly behind.

Gas! GAS! Quick, boys!—An ecstasy of fumbling,
Fitting the clumsy helmets just in time,
But someone still was yelling out and stumbling
And floundering like a man in fire or lime.——
Dim through the misty panes and thick green light,
As under a green sea, I saw him drowning.

In all my dreams before my helpless sight
He plunges at me, guttering, choking, drowning.

If in some smothering dreams, you too could pace
Behind the wagon that we flung him in,
And watch the white eyes writhing in his face,
His hanging face, like a devil's sick of sin;
If you could hear, at every jolt, the blood
Come gargling from the froth-corrupted lungs,
Bitter as the cud
Of vile, incurable sores on innocent tongues,——
My friend, you would not tell with such high zest
To children ardent for some desperate glory,
The old Lie: Dulce et decorum est
Pro patria mori.

Wilfred Owen

Bombing Casualties: Spain

Dolls' faces are rosier but these were children
their eyes not glass but gleaming gristle
dark lenses in whose quick silvery glances
the sunlight quivered. These blenched lips
were warm once and bright with blood
but blood
held in a moist bleb of flesh
not spilt and spatter'd in tousled hair.

In these shadowy tresses
red petals did not always
thus clot and blacken to a scar.

These are dead faces:
wasps' nests are not more wanly waxen
wood embers not so greyly ashen.

They are laid out in ranks
like paper lanterns that have fallen
after a night of riot
extinct in the dry morning air.

Herbert Read

Then

There were no men and women then at all,
But the flesh lying alone,
And angry shadows fighting on a wall
That now and then sent out a groan
Buried in lime and stone,
And sweated now and then like tortured wood
Big drops that looked yet did not not look like blood.

And yet as each drop came a shadow faded
And left the wall.
There was a lull
Until another in its shadow arrayed it,
Came, fought and left a blood-mark on the wall;
And that was all; the blood was all.

If there had been women there they might have wept
For the poor blood, unowned, unwanted,
Blank as forgotten script.
The wall was haunted
By mute maternal presences whose sighing
Fluttered the fighting shadows and shook the wall
As if that fury of death itself were dying.

Edwin Muir

Further Reading

KARL SHAPIRO. The Conscientious Objector. *Collected Poems*, Random House; or *Oxford Book of American Verse*.

RANDALL JARRELL. Eighth Air Force; Losses. *Losses*, Harcourt, Brace; or *Modern Verse in English 1900–50*, Eyre and Spottiswoode.

WILFRED OWEN. Exposure; Spring Offensive. *The Collected Poems of Wilfred Owen*, Chatto and Windus; or *Modern Verse in English 1900–50*, Eyre and Spottiswoode.

SIEGFRIED SASSOON. Counter-Attack. *Flash Point*, E. J. Arnold.

DYLAN THOMAS. Among those killed in the dawn raid was a man aged a hundred. *Collected Poems*, Dent; or *Anthology of Modern Poetry*, Hutchinson.

ISAAC ROSENBERG. Dead Man's Dump; Break of Day in the Trenches, *Collected Poems*, Chatto and Windus; or *The Faber Book of Modern Verse*.

LOUIS MACNEICE. The Streets of Laredo. *Collected Poems*, Faber; or *Flash Point*, E. J. Arnold.

CECIL DAY LEWIS. Will it be so again? *Word over All*, Cape; or *Modern Verse 1900–50*, Oxford University Press, World's Classics.

12 *Pain*

I Look into my Glass

I look into my glass,
And view my wasting skin,
And say, 'Would God it came to pass
My heart had shrunk as thin!'

For then, I, undistrest
By hearts grown cold to me,
Could lonely wait my endless rest
With equanimity.

But Time, to make me grieve,
Part steals, lets part abide;
And shakes this fragile frame at eve
With throbbings of noontide.

Thomas Hardy

Gulliver

I'll kick your wall to bits, I'll die scratching a tunnel,
If you'll give me a wall, if you'll give me simple stone,
If you'll do me the honour of a dungeon—
Anything but this tyranny of sinews.
Lashed with a hundred ropes of nerve and bone
I lie, poor helpless Gulliver,
In a twopenny dock for the want of a penny,
Tied up with stuff too cheap, and strings too many.
One chain is usually sufficient for a cur.

Hair over hair, I pick my cables loose,
But still the ridiculous manacles confine me.
I snap them, swollen with sobbing. What's the use?
One hair I break, ten thousand hairs entwine me.
Love, hunger, drunkenness, neuralgia, debt,
Cold weather, hot weather, sleep and age—
If I could only unloose their spongy fingers,
I'd have a chance yet, slip through the cage.
But who ever heard of a cage of hairs?
You can't scrape tunnels in a net.

If you'd give me a chain, if you'd give me honest iron,
If you'd graciously give me a turnkey,
I could break my teeth on a chain, I could bite through metal,
But what can you do with hairs?
For God's sake, call the hangman.

Kenneth Slessor

African Beggar

Sprawled in the dust outside the Syrian store,
a target for small children, dogs and flies,
a heap of verminous rags and matted hair,
he watches us with cunning, reptile eyes,
his noseless, smallpoxed face creased in a sneer.

Sometimes he shows his yellow stumps of teeth
and whines for alms, perceiving that we bear
the curse of pity; a grotesque mask of death,
with hands like claws about his begging-bowl.

But often he is lying all alone
within the shadow of a crumbling wall,
lost in the trackless jungle of his pain,
clutching the pitiless red earth in vain
and whimpering like a stricken animal.

Raymond Tong

from *King Oedipus*

Her death was hidden from us.
Before we could see out her tragedy,
The King broke in with piercing cries, and all
Had eyes only for him. This way and that
He strode among us. 'A sword, a sword!' he cried;
'Where is that wife, no wife of mine—that soil
Where I was sown, and whence I reaped my harvest!'
While thus he raved, some demon guided him—
For none of us dared speak—to where she was.
As if in answer to some leader's call
With wild hallooing cries he hurled himself
Upon the locked doors, bending by main force
The bolts out of their sockets—and stumbled in.

We saw a knotted pendulum, a noose,
A strangled woman swinging before our eyes.

The King saw too, and with heart-rending groans
Untied the rope, and laid her on the ground.
But worse was yet to see. Her dress was pinned
With golden brooches, which the King snatched out
And thrust, from full arm's length, into his eyes—
Eyes that should see no longer his shame, his guilt,
No longer see those they should never have seen,
Nor see, unseeing, those he had longed to see,
Henceforth seeing nothing but night. . . . To this wild tune
He pierced his eyeballs time and time again,
Till bloody tears ran down his beard—not drops
But in full spate a whole cascade descending
In drenching cataracts of scarlet rain.

Sophocles
translated by E. F. Watling

Written in Northampton County Asylum

I am! yet what I am who cares, or knows?
  My friends forsake me like a memory lost.
I am the self-consumer of my woes;
  They rise and vanish, an oblivious host,
Shadows of life, whose very soul is lost.
And yet I am—I live—though I am tossed

Into the nothingness of scorn and noise,
  Into the living sea of waking dream,
Where there is neither sense of life, nor joys,
  But the huge shipwreck of my own esteem
And all that's dear. Even those I loved the best
Are strange—nay, they are stranger than the rest.

I long for scenes where man has never trod—
  For scenes where woman never smiled or wept—
There to abide with my Creator, God,
  And sleep as I in childhood sweetly slept,
Full of high thoughts, unborn. So let me lie—
The grass below; above, the vaulted sky.

John Clare

Further Reading

GERARD MANLEY HOPKINS. No Worst, There is None; I Wake and Feel the Fell of Dark. *Poems of Gerard Manley Hopkins*, Oxford University Press; or *Flash Point*, E. J. Arnold.

THOMAS BLACKBURN. Oedipus. *A Smell of Burning*, Putnam.

ANTHONY HECHT. The Place of Pain in the Universe. *A Summoning of Stones*, Macmillan; or *The Faber Book of Modern American Verse*.

EDWIN ARLINGTON ROBINSON. Richard Cory. *The Children of the Night*, Scribner; or *Modern Verse in English 1900–50*, Eyre and Spottiswoode.

EMILY DICKINSON. After great pain, a formal feeling comes. *The Poems of Emily Dickinson*, Little, Brown; or *Modern Verse in English 1900–50*, Eyre and Spottiswoode.

DYLAN THOMAS. 'Out of the sighs . . .'. *Collected Poems*, Dent; or *Modern Verse, 1900–50*, Oxford University Press, World's Classics.

EMILY BRONTË. Sleep Brings No Joy. *The Mentor Book of Major British Poets*.

ALAN PORTER. The Signature of Pain. *The Signature of Pain*, Cobden-Sanderson; or *Poems of Our Time 1900–1960*, Dent.

13 Love

First Love

I ne'er was struck before that hour
   With love so sudden and so sweet,
Her face it bloomed like a sweet flower
   And stole my heart away complete.
My face turned pale as deadly pale,
   My legs refused to walk away,
And when she looked, what could I ail?
   My life and all seemed turned to clay.

And then my blood rushed to my face
   And took my eyesight quite away,
The trees and bushes round the place
   Seemed midnight at noonday.
I could not see a single thing,
   Words from my eyes did start—
They spoke as chords do from the string,
   And blood burnt round my heart.

Are flowers the winter's choice?
   Is love's bed always snow?
She seemed to hear my silent voice,
   Not love's appeals to know.
I never saw so sweet a face
   As that I stood before.
My heart has left its dwelling place
   And can return no more.

John Clare

Black Monday Lovesong

In love's dances, in love's dances
One retreats and one advances.
One grows warmer and one colder,
One more hesitant, one bolder.
One gives what the other needed
Once, or will need, now unheeded.
One is clenched, compact, ingrowing
While the other's melting, flowing.
One is smiling and concealing
While the other's asking, kneeling.
One is arguing or sleeping
While the other's weeping, weeping.

And the question finds no answer
And the time misleads the dancer
And the lost look finds no other
And the lost hand finds no brother
And the word is left unspoken
Till the theme and thread are broken.

When shall these divisions alter?
Echo's answer seems to falter:
'Oh the unperplexed, unvexed time
Next time . . . one day . . . one day . . . next time!'

A. S. J. Tessimond

In a Bath Teashop

'Let us not speak, for the love we bear one another—
  Let us hold hands and look.'
She, such a very ordinary little woman;
  He, such a thumping crook;
But both, for a moment, little lower than the angels
  In the teashop's ingle-nook.

John Betjeman

One Flesh

Lying apart now, each in a separate bed,
He with a book, keeping the light on late,
She like a girl dreaming of childhood,
All men elsewhere—it is as if they wait
Some new event: the book he holds unread,
Her eyes fixed on the shadows overhead.

Tossed up like flotsam from a former passion,
How cool they lie. They hardly ever touch,
Or if they do it is like a confession
Of having little feeling—or too much.
Chastity faces them, a destination
For which their whole lives were a preparation.

Strangely apart and strangely close together,
Silence between them like a thread to hold
And not wind in. And time itself's a feather
Touching them gently. Do they know they're old,
These two who are my father and my mother
Whose fire, from which I came, has now grown cold?

Elizabeth Jennings

His being was in her alone

His being was in her alone:
And he not being, she was none.

They joyed one joy, one grief they grieved;
One love they loved, one life they lived.
The hand was one, one was the sword,
That did his death, her death afford.

As all the rest, so now the stone
That tombs the two is justly one.

Sir Philip Sidney

Further Reading

JOHN LOGAN. The Picnic. *Ghosts of the Heart*, University of Chicago Press.

KINGSLEY AMIS. A Dream of Fair Women. *A Case of Samples*, Gollancz; or *The New Poetry*. Penguin.

TED HUGHES. The Decay of Vanity. *The Hawk in the Rain*, Faber; or *New Voices*, Vista Books, The Pocket Poets.

ROBERT LOWELL. 'To Speak of the Woe that is in Marriage.' *Poems 1938–49*, Faber; or *The New Poetry*, Penguin.

W. H. AUDEN. Lay Your Sleeping Head, My Love. *Collected Poems*, Faber; or *Modern Verse in English 1900–50*, Eyre and Spottiswoode.

PHILIP LARKIN. Wedding Wind. *The Less Deceived*, Marvell Press; or *The New Poetry*, Penguin.

D. H. LAWRENCE. The Young Wife. *Collected Poems of D. H. Lawrence*, Heinemann.

DAVID WRIGHT. Upon a Marriage Anniversary. *Monologue of a Deaf Man*, Deutsch.

ANTHONY CRONIN. The Lover. *Poems*, Cresset Press; or *45–60: An Anthology of English Poetry 1945–60*, Putnam.

GEORGE BARKER. To My Mother. *Eros in Dogma*, Faber; or *The Faber Book of Modern Verse*.

14 *Experience*

Wires

The widest prairies have electric fences,
For though old cattle know they must not stray,
Young steers are always scenting purer water
Not here but anywhere. Beyond the wires

Leads them to blunder up against the wires
Whose muscle-shredding violence gives no quarter.
Young steers become old cattle from that day,
Electric limits to their widest senses.

Philip Larkin

I stepped from plank to plank

I stepped from plank to plank
   So slow and cautiously;
The stars about my head I felt,
   About my feet the sea.

I knew not but the next
   Would be my final inch,—
This gave me that precarious gait
   Some call experience.

Emily Dickinson

The One Furrow

When I was young, I went to school
With pencil and foot-rule
Sponge and slate,
And sat on a tall stool
At learning's gate.

When I was older, the gate swung wide;
Clever and keen-eyed
In I pressed,
But found in the mind's pride
No peace, no rest.

Then who was it taught me back to go
To cattle and barrow,
Field and plough;
To keep to the one furrow,
As I do now?

R. S. Thomas

The State of Man

This is the state of man: today he puts forth
The tender leaves of hope; tomorrow blossoms,
And bears his blushing honours thick upon him;
The third day comes a frost, a killing frost,
And,—when he thinks, good easy man, full surely
His greatness is a-ripening,—nips his root,
And then he falls as I do. I have ventur'd,
Like little wanton boys that swim on bladders,
This many summers in a sea of glory;
But far beyond my depth: my high-blown pride
At length broke under me; and now has left me,
Weary and old with service, to the mercy
Of a rude stream, that must forever hide me.

William Shakespeare
KING HENRY VIII

Further Reading

EDMUND BLUNDEN. Report on Experience. *Poems*, Macmillan; or *Flash Point*, E. J. Arnold.

E. E. CUMMINGS. plato told. *Poems 1923–1955*, Brandt and Brandt; or *E. E. Cummings*, Penguin Poets.

THOMAS HARDY. On his 86th Birthday. *Collected Poems of Thomas Hardy*, Macmillan; or *An Anthology of Commonwealth Verse*, Blackie.

STEPHEN SPENDER. What I expected. *Collected Poems*, Faber; or *Anthology of Modern Poetry*, Hutchinson.

DOM MORAES. Words to a Boy. *New Voices*, Vista Books, Pocket Poets.

RICHARD KELL. Innocence, from *Control Tower*, Chatto and Windus; or *Flash Point*, E. J. Arnold.

WILLIAM SHAKESPEARE. There,—my blessing with you. *Hamlet*, Act I, Scene 3, lines 57–80.

JOHN CROWE RANSOM. Old Man Playing with Children. *Selected Poems*, Eyre and Spottiswoode; or *Anthology of Modern Poetry*, Hutchinson.

15 Work

Toads

Why should I let the toad *work*
 Squat on my life?
Can't I use my wit as a pitchfork
 And drive the brute off?

Six days of the week it soils
 With its sickening poison—
Just for paying a few bills!
 That's out of proportion.

Lots of folk live on their wits:
 Lecturers, lispers,
Losels, loblolly-men, louts—
 They don't end as paupers.

Lots of folk live up lanes
 With a fire in a bucket;
Eat windfalls and sardines—
 They seem to like it.

Their nippers have got bare feet,
 Their unspeakable wives
Are skinny as whippets—and yet
 No one actually *starves*.

Ah, were I courageous enough
 To shout *Stuff your pension!*
But I know, all too well, that's the stuff
 That dreams are made on:

For something sufficiently toad-like
 Squats in me too;
Its hunkers are heavy as hard luck,
 And cold as snow,

And will never allow me to blarney
  My way to getting
The fame and the girl and the money
  All at one sitting.

I don't say, one bodies the other
  One's spiritual truth;
But I do say it's hard to lose either,
  When you have both.

Philip Larkin

Work

There is no point in work
  unless it absorbs you
  like an absorbing game.

If it doesn't absorb you
  if it's never any fun,
  don't do it.

When a man goes out into his work
he is alive like a tree in spring,
he is living, not merely working.

When the Hindus weave thin wool into long, long lengths of
  stuff
With their thin dark hands and their wide dark eyes and their souls
  still absorbed
they are like slender trees putting forth leaves, a long white web
  of living leaf,
        the tissue they weave,
and they clothe themselves in white as a tree clothes itself in its
  own foliage.

As with cloth, so with houses, ships, shoes, wagons or cups or
  loaves.
Men might put them forth as a snail its shell, as a bird that leans
        its breast against its nest, to make it round,
as the turnip models his round root, as the bush makes flowers or
  gooseberries,
        putting them forth, not manufacturing them,
and cities might be as once they were, bowers grown out from
  the busy bodies of people.
And so it will be again, men will smash the machines.

At last, for the sake of clothing himself in his own leaf-like cloth
      tissued from his life,
And dwelling in his own bowery house, like a beaver's nibbled
    mansion
And drinking from cups that came off his fingers like flowers off
    their five-fold stem
he will cancel the machines we have got.

D. H. Lawrence

Au Jardin des Plantes

The gorilla lay on his back,
One hand cupped under his head,
Like a man.

Like a labouring man tired with work,
A strong man with his strength burnt away
In the toil of earning a living.

Only of course he was not tired out with work,
Merely with boredom; his terrible strength
All burnt away with prodigal idleness.

A thousand days, and then a thousand days,
Idleness licked away his beautiful strength,
He having no need to earn a living.

It was all laid on, free of charge.
We maintained him, not for doing anything,
But for being what he was.

And so that Sunday morning he lay on his back,
Like a man, like a worn-out man,
One hand cupped under his terrible hard head.

Like a man, like a man,
One of those we maintain, not for doing anything,
But for being what they are.

A thousand days, and then a thousand days,
With everything laid on, free of charge,
They cup their heads in prodigal idleness.

John Wain

Martha of Bethany

It's all very well
Sitting in the shade of the courtyard
Talking about your souls.
Someone's got to see to the cooking,
Standing at the oven all morning
With you two taking your ease.
It's all very well
Saying he'd be content
With bread and honey.
Perhaps he would—but I wouldn't,
Coming to our house like this,
Not giving him of our best.
Yes, it's all very well
Him trying to excuse you,
Saying your recipe's best,
Saying that I worry too much,
That I'm always anxious.
Someone's got to worry—
And double if the others don't care.
For it's all very well
Talking of faith and belief,
But what would you do
If everyone sat in the cool
Not getting their meals?
And he can't go wandering and preaching
On an empty stomach—
He'd die in the first fortnight.
Then where would you be
With all your discussions and questions
And no one to answer them? It's all very well.

Clive Sansom

Further Reading

PHILIP LARKIN. Toads Revisited. *The Whitsun Weddings*, Faber.

WILFRED OWEN. Miners. *The Collected Works of Wilfred Owen*, Chatto and Windus; or *The Mentor Book of Major British Poets*.

EDWARD ARLINGTON ROBINSON. The Clerks. *Children of the Night*, Scribner; or *Modern Verse in English 1900–50*, Eyre and Spottiswoode.

ROBERT FROST. The Death of the Hired Man; A Lone Striker. *The Complete Works of Robert Frost*, Cape; or *Robert Frost*, The Penguin Poets.

HAROLD MONRO. Man carrying Bale. *Collected Poems*, Cobden-Sanderson.

TANER BAYBARS. The Oracle. *To Catch a Falling Man*, Scorpion Press; or *A Group Anthology*, Oxford University Press.

VERNON WATKINS. The Collier. *Modern Verse in English 1900–1950*, Eyre and Spottiswoode.

NORMAN NICHOLSON. Cleator Moor. *Five Rivers*, Faber; or *Flash Point*, E. J. Arnold.

16 *Leisure*

Sunday Morning

Down the road someone is practising scales,
The notes like little fishes vanish with a wink of tails,
Man's heart expands to tinker with his car
For this is Sunday morning, Fate's great bazaar,
Regard these means as ends, concentrate on this Now,
And you may grow to music or drive beyond Hindhead anyhow,
Take corners on two wheels until you go so fast
That you can clutch a fringe or two of the windy past,
That you can abstract this day and make it to the week of time
A small eternity, a sonnet self-contained in rhyme.

But listen, up the road, something gulps, the church spire
Opens its eight bells out, skulls' mouths which will not tire
To tell how there is no music or movement which secures
Escape from the weekday time. Which deadens and endures.

Louis MacNeice

Rugby League Game

Sport is absurd, and sad.
Those grown men, just look,
In those dreary long blue shorts,
Those ringed stockings, Edwardian,
Balding pates, and huge
Fat knees that ought to be heroes'.

Grappling, hooking, gallantly tackling—
Is all this courage really necessary?—
Taking their good clean fun
So solemnly, they run each other down
With earnest keenness, for the honour of
Virility, the cap, the county side.

Like great boys they roll each other
In the mud of public Saturdays,
Groping their blind way back
To noble youth, away from the bank,
The wife, the pram, the spin drier,
Back to the spartan freedom of the field.

Back, back to the days when boys
Were men, still hopeful, and untamed,
That was then: a gay
And golden age ago.
Now, in vain, domesticated,
Men try to be boys again.

James Kirkup

Public Library

Who, in the public library, one evening after rain,
amongst the polished tables and linoleum,
stands bored under blank light to glance at these pages?
Whose absent mood, like neon glowing in the night,
is conversant with wet pavements, nothing to do?

Neutral, the clock-watching girl stamps out the date,
a forced celebration, a posthumous birthday,
her head buttered by the drizzling library lamps;
yet the accident of words, too, can light the semi-dark
should the reader lead them home, generously journey,
later to return, perhaps leaving a bus ticket as a bookmark.

Who wrote in margins hieroglyphic notations,
that obscenity, deleted this imperfect line?
Read by whose hostile eyes, in what bed-sitting rooms,
in which rainy, dejected railway stations?

Dannie Abse

High Flight

Oh! I have slipped the surly bonds of earth
   And danced the skies on laughter-silvered wings;
Sunward I've climbed, and joined the tumbling mirth
   Of sun-split clouds—and done a hundred things
You have not dreamed of—wheeled and soared and swung
   High in the sun-lit silence. Hov'ring there
I've chased the shouting wind along, and flung
   My eager craft thro' footless halls of air.

Up, up the long, delirious, burning blue
   I've topped the wind-swept heights with easy grace
Where never lark, nor even eagle flew—
   And while with silent, lifting mind I've trod
The high, untrespassed sanctity of space,
   Put out my hand and touched the face of God.

John Gillespie Magee

Happiness

I asked professors who teach the meaning of life to tell me what
  is happiness.
And I went to famous executives who boss the work of thousands
  of men.
They all shook their heads and gave me a smile as though I was
  trying to fool with them.
And then one Sunday afternoon I wandered out along the Des-
  plaines river
And I saw a crowd of Hungarians under the trees with their
  women and children and a keg of beer and an accordion.

Carl Sandburg

Further Reading

JOHN BETJEMAN. Beside the Seaside. *Collected Poems*, Murray.

JAMES KIRKUP. Nippon's Non-stop Nudes. *Refusal to Conform*, Oxford University Press.

LOUIS MACNEICE. Indoor Sports. *Solstices*, Faber.

PHYLLIS MACGINLEY. Country Club Sunday. *A Short Walk to the Station*, Viking; or *The Faber Book of Modern American Verse*.

DELMORE SCHWARTZ. 'All of us always turning away for solace.' *Oxford Book of American Verse*, Oxford University Press.

THOMAS GUNN. Elvis Presley; Black Jackets. *The Sense of Movement*, Faber; or *The New Poetry*, Penguin.

EMILY DICKINSON. I Taste a Liquor Never Brewed. *Poems of Emily Dickinson*, Little, Brown; or *The Modern Poet's World*, Heinemann.

MARTIN BELL. Fiesta Mask. *Penguin Modern Poets 3*; or *A Group Anthology*, Oxford University Press.

DOM MORAES. One of Us. *Poems 1960*, Eyre and Spottiswoode; or *Penguin Modern Poets 2*.

D. H. LAWRENCE. When I went to the Circus. *Collected Poems of D. H. Lawrence*, Heinemann; or *The Mentor Book of Major British Poets*.

17 Contemporary Man

The Man in the Bowler Hat

I am the unnoticed, the unnoticeable man:
The man who sat on your right in the morning train:
The man you looked through like a windowpane:
The man who was the colour of the carriage, the colour of the
    mounting
Morning pipe smoke.

I am the man too busy with a living to live,
Too hurried and worried to see and smell and touch:
The man who is patient too long and obeys too much
And wishes too softly and seldom.

I am the man they call the nation's backbone,
Who am boneless—playable catgut, pliable clay:
The Man they label Little lest one day
I dare to grow.

I am the rails on which the moment passes,
The megaphone for many words and voices:
I am graph, diagram,
Composite face.

I am the led, the easily-fed,
The tool, the not-quite-fool,
The would-be-safe-and-sound,
The uncomplaining, bound,
The dust fine-ground,
Stone-for-a-statue waveworn pebble-round.

A. S. J. Tessimond

The Unknown Citizen

(*To JS/o7/M378 This Marble Monument is Erected by the State*)

He was found by the Bureau of Statistics to be
One against whom there was no official complaint,
And all the reports on his conduct agree
That, in the modern sense of an old-fashioned word, he was a
    saint,
For in everything he did he served the Greater Community.
Except for the War till the day he retired
He worked in a factory and never got fired,
But satisfied his employers, Fudge Motors Inc.
Yet he wasn't a scab or odd in his views,
For his Union reports that he paid his dues,
(Our report on his Union shows it was sound)
And our Social Psychology workers found
That he was popular with his mates and liked a drink.
The Press are convinced that he bought a paper every day
And that his reactions to advertisements were normal in every
    way.
Policies taken out in his name prove that he was fully insured,
And his Health-card shows that he was once in hospital but left it
    cured.
Both Producers Research and High-Grade Living declare
He was fully sensible to the advantages of the Instalment Plan
And had everything necessary to the Modern Man,
A phonograph, a radio, a car and a frigidaire.
Our researchers into Public Opinion are content
That he held the proper opinions for the time of year;
When there was peace, he was for peace; when there was war, he
    went.
He was married and added five children to the population,
Which our Eugenist says was the right number for a parent of his
    generation,

And our teachers report that he never interfered with their
   education.
Was he free? Was he happy? The question is absurd:
Had anything been wrong, we should certainly have heard.

W. H. Auden

The Planster's Vision

Cut down that timber! Bells, too many and strong,
Pouring their music through the branches bare,
From moon-white church-towers down the windy air
Have pealed the centuries out with Evensong.
Remove those cottages, a huddled throng!
Too many babies have been born in there,
Too many coffins, bumping down the stair,
Carried the old their garden paths along.

I have a Vision of the Future, chum,
The workers' flats in fields of soya beans
Tower up like silver pencils, score on score:
And Surging Millions hear the Challenge come
From microphones in communal canteens
'No Right! No Wrong! All's perfect, evermore.'

John Betjeman

Song of the Twentieth-century Man

from the German of Jura Soyfer

Human we were counted once, perhaps,
Or one far-off day we may be so
When we've found an answer to these traps;
But, here and now, to call us human? No.

We're just a name that's written on a pass,
A dumb reflection in a looking glass,
The echo of what once was finely said,
The rumour of a rumour that's long dead.

What was human long ago stamped out—
Why should we keep up the empty show?
In our faceless cities swirled about
Shall we still pretend we're human? No.

We are the dust that's blown from lamp to lamp,
The queue that waits for the official stamp,
The number in a bureaucratic file,
And our own shadows could not be more vile.

A poor, half-finished sketch is all we are
A glimpse of humans in their finished state,
A tune suggested by the opening bar—
You call us wretches human beings? Wait!

John Lehmann

Further Reading

E. E. CUMMINGS. pity this busy monster, manunkind. *Poems 1923–1955*, Brandt and Brandt; or *Modern Verse in English 1900–50*, Eyre and Spottiswoode.

ROBINSON JEFFERS. Summer Holiday; Shine, Perishing Republic. *Roan Stallion*, Random House; or *Modern Verse in English 1900–50*, Eyre and Spottiswoode.

JOHN BETJEMAN. Business Girls. *Collected Poems*, Murray; or *45–60: An Anthology of English Poetry 1945–60*, Putnam.

D. J. ENRIGHT. No Offence: Berlin. *Some Men are Brothers*, Chatto and Windus; or *45–60: An Anthology of English Poetry 1945–60*, Putnam.

K. W. GRANSDEN. The Room. *New Voices*, Vista Books, Pocket Poets.

DAVID WEVILL. The Space Flier. *A Group Anthology*, Oxford University Press.

JAMES SIMMONS. Leeds 2. *Flash Point*, E. J. Arnold.

A. S. J. TESSIMOND. A Man of Culture. *The Harrap Book of Modern Verse*.

T. S. ELIOT. The Hollow Men. *Collected Poems*, Faber; or *Flash Point*, E. J. Arnold.

D. H. LAWRENCE. Let Us be Men. *Collected Poems*, Heinemann; or *The Modern Poet's World*, Heinemann.

18 Your Attention Please

This Excellent Machine

This excellent machine is neatly planned,
A child, a half-wit would not feel perplexed:
No chance to err, you simply press the button—
At once each cog in motion moves the next,
The whole revolves, and anything that lives
Is quickly sucked towards the running band,
Where, shot between the automatic knives,
It's guaranteed to finish dead as mutton.

This excellent machine will illustrate
The modern world divided into nations:
So neatly planned, that if you merely tap it
The armaments will start their devastations,
And though we're for it, though we're all convinced
Some fool will press the button soon or late,
We stand and stare, expecting to be minced—
And very few are asking *Why not scrap it?*

John Lehmann

Your Attention Please

The Polar DEW has just warned that
A nuclear rocket strike of
At least one thousand megatons
Has been launched by the enemy
Directly at our major cities.
This announcement will take
Two and a quarter minutes to make,
You therefore have a further
Eight and a quarter minutes
To comply with the shelter
Requirements published in the Civil
Defence Code—section Atomic Attack.
A specially shortened Mass
Will be broadcast at the end
Of this announcement—
Protestant and Jewish services
Will begin simultaneously—
Select your wavelength immediately
According to instructions
In the Defence Code. Do not
Take well-loved pets (including birds)
Into your shelter—they will consume
Fresh air. Leave the old and bed-
ridden, you can do nothing for them.
Remember to press the sealing
Switch when everyone is in
The shelter. Set the radiation
Aerial, turn on the geiger barometer.
Turn off your Television now.
Turn off your radio immediately
The Services end. At the same time
Secure explosion plugs in the ears
Of each member of your family. Take
Down your plasma flasks. Give your children
The pills marked one and two

In the C.D. green container, then put
Them to bed. Do not break
The inside airlock seals until
The radiation All Clear shows
(Watch for the cuckoo in your
perspex panel), or your District
Touring Doctor rings your bell.
If before this, your air becomes
Exhausted or if any of your family
Is critically injured, administer
The capsules marked 'Valley Forge'
(Red pocket in No. 1 Survival Kit)
For painless death. (Catholics
Will have been instructed by their priests
What to do in this eventuality.)
This announcement is ending. Our President
Has already given orders for
Massive retaliation—it will be
Decisive. Some of us may die.
Remember, statistically
It is not likely to be you.
All flags are flying fully dressed
On Government buildings—the sun is shining.
Death is the least we have to fear.
We are all in the hands of God,
Whatever happens happens by His Will.
Now go quickly to your shelters.

Peter Porter

The horses

Barely a twelvemonth after
The seven days war that put the world to sleep,
Late in the evening the strange horses came.
By then we had made our covenant with silence,
But in the first few days it was so still
We listened to our breathing and were afraid.
On the second day
The radios failed; we turned the knobs; no answer.
On the third day a warship passed us, heading north,
Dead bodies piled on the deck. On the sixth day
A plane plunged over us into the sea. Thereafter
Nothing. The radios dumb;
And still they stand in corners of our kitchens,
And stand, perhaps, turned on, in a million rooms
All over the world. But now if they should speak,
If on a sudden they should speak again,
If on the stroke of noon a voice should speak,
We would not listen, we would not let it bring
That old bad world that swallowed its children quick
At one great gulp. We would not have it again.
Sometimes we think of the nations lying asleep,
Curled blindly in impenetrable sorrow,
And then the thought confounds us with its strangeness.

The tractors lie about our fields; at evening
They look like dank sea-monsters couched and waiting.
We leave them where they are and let them rust:
'They'll moulder away and be like other loam.'
We make our oxen drag our rusty ploughs,
Long laid aside. We have gone back
Far past our fathers' land.
                          And then, that evening
Late in the summer the strange horses came.
We heard a distant tapping on the road,
A deepening drumming; it stopped, went on again.

And at the corner changed to hollow thunder.
We saw the heads
Like a wild wave charging and were afraid.
We had sold our horses in our fathers' time
To buy new tractors. Now they were strange to us
As fabulous steeds set on an ancient shield
Or illustrations in a book of knights.
We did not dare go near them. Yet they waited,
Stubborn and shy, as if they had been sent
By an old command to find our whereabouts
And that long-lost archaic companionship.
In the first moment we had never thought
That they were creatures to be owned and used.
Among them were some half-a-dozen colts
Dropped in some wilderness of the broken world,
Yet new as if they had come from their own Eden.
Since then they have pulled our ploughs and borne our loads,
But that free servitude still can pierce our hearts.
Our life is changed; their coming our beginning.

Edwin Muir

After a hundred years

After a hundred years
Nobody knows the place,—
Agony, that enacted there,
Motionless as peace.

Weeds triumphant ranged,
Strangers strolled and spelled
At the lone orthography
Of the elder dead.

Winds of summer fields
Recollect the way,—
Instinct picking up the key
Dropped by memory.

Emily Dickinson

God's Grandeur

The world is charged with the grandeur of God.
　　It will flame out, like shining from shook foil;
　　It gathers to a greatness, like the ooze of oil
Crushed. Why do men then now not reck his rod?
Generations have trod, have trod, have trod;
　　And all is seared with trade; bleared, smeared with toil;
　　And wears man's smudge and shares man's smell: the soil
Is bare now, nor can foot feel, being shod.

And for all this, nature is never spent;
　　There lives the dearest freshness deep down things;
And though the last lights off the black West went
　　Oh, morning, at the brown brink eastward, springs—
Because the Holy Ghost over the bent
　　World broods with warm breast and with ah! bright wings.

Gerard Manley Hopkins

Further Reading

THOMAS BLACKBURN. Bombs. *A Smell of Burning*, Putnam.

MICHAEL BALDWIN. After the Bang. *Death on a Live Wire*, Longmans.

CARL SANDBURG. Grass. *Chicago Poems*, Henry Holt; or *Modern Verse in English 1900–50*, Eyre and Spottiswoode.

ROBERT FROST. The Planners. *The Complete Works*, Cape; or *Robert Frost*, Penguin Poets.

ALEXANDER BAIRD. Hiroshima Sunset. *Poems*, Chatto and Windus.

JAMES KIRKUP. No More Hiroshimas. *Refusal to Conform*, Oxford University Press.

D. J. ENRIGHT. Monuments of Hiroshima. *The Laughing Hyena*, Routledge.

GEOFFREY GRIGSON. New Mexican Desert. *Collected Poems*, Phoenix.

ALAN BROWNJOHN. William Empson at Aldermaston. *The Railings*, Digby Press; or *A Group Anthology*, Oxford University Press.

ADRIAN MITCHELL. Veteran with a Head Wound. *A Group Anthology*, Oxford University Press.

EDITH SITWELL. Dirge for the new sunrise. *Collected Poems*, Macmillan; or *Edith Sitwell*, Penguin Poets.

Book List

The following list has been compiled as an aid to further study and contains:

1. A select list of anthologies.
2. A short list of paperback anthologies.
3. Details of Longmans Poetry Library.
4. Books by individual poets.
5. Surveys.

1. Anthologies

AUDEN, W. H., ed. *The Faber Book of Modern American Verse*, Faber.

BLACKBURN, T., ed. *An Anthology of English Poetry, 1945–60*, Putnam.

CECIL, D. and TATE, A., eds. *Modern Verse in English, 1900–50*, Eyre and Spottiswoode.

CONQUEST, R., ed. *New Lines*, Macmillan.

FRASER, G. S., ed. *Poetry Now*, Faber.

JENNINGS, E., ed. *An Anthology of Modern Verse, 1940–1960*, Methuen.

MATTHIESSEN, F., ed. *The Oxford Book of American Verse*, Oxford University Press.

O'DONNELL, M., ed. *An Anthology of Commonwealth Verse*, Blackie.

QUILLER-COUCH, SIR A., ed. *The Oxford Book of English Verse 1250–1918*, Oxford University Press.

REEVES, J., ed. *The Modern Poet's World*, Heinemann.

ROBERTS, M., ed. *The Faber Book of Modern Verse*.

SHAW, R., ed. *Flash Point*, E. J. Arnold.

WAIN, J., ed. *Anthology of Modern Poetry*, Hutchinson.

The Guiness Book of Poetry. Annually from 1956–57.

P.E.N., *New Poems*. Annually from 1952.

2. Paperback Anthologies

ALLOTT, K., ed. *Contemporary Verse*, Penguin.

ALVAREZ, A., ed. *The New Poetry*, Penguin.

HALL, D. ed. *Contemporary American Poetry*, Penguin.

PRYCE-JONES, A., ed. *New Voices*, Vista Books, Pocket Poets.

SILKIN, J. ed. *Living Voices*, Vista Books, Pocket Poets.

WILLIAMS, O., ed. *The Mentor Book of Major British Poets*, The New English Library.

WILLIAMS, O., ed. *The Mentor Book of Major American Poets*, The New English Library.

Penguin Modern Poets, 1–6. Penguin.

3. *Longmans Poetry Library*

Editor: Leonard Clark

Grey Books (suitable for pupils from 13 to 18 years).

DYLAN THOMAS AND ANDREW YOUNG

ROBERT GRAVES AND D. H. LAWRENCE

WORDSWORTH

MATTHEW ARNOLD

LOVE

FEAR

WILD AND TAME

FOLKSONGS AND BALLADS

4. *Individual Poets*

ABSE, D. *Tenants of the House; Poems, Golders Green*, Hutchinson.

BLACKBURN, T. *The Outer Darkness; The Holy Stone*, Hand and Flowers. *In the Fire; The Next Word; A Smell of Burning*, Putnam.

FULLER, R. *Poems*, Fortune. *The Middle of a War; A Lost Season*, Hogarth. *Epitaphs and Occasions*, Lehmann. *Counterparts*, Verschoyle. *Brutus's Orchard*, Deutsch. *Collected Poems*, Deutsch.

GASCOYNE, D. *Man's Life is this Meat*, Parton. *Poems 1937–42*, Poetry London. *A Vagrant*, Lehmann. *Night Thoughts*, Deutsch.

HALL, J. C. *The Summer Dance*, Lehmann.

HOLBROOK, D. *Imaginings*, Putnam.

HUGHES, T. *The Hawk in the Rain; Lupercal*, Faber.

JENNINGS, E. *A Way of Looking; A Sense of the World; Poems for a Birth or a Death*, Deutsch.

KUNITZ, S. *Selected Poems*, Dent.

LARKIN, P. *The North Ship*, Fortune Press. *The Less Deceived*, Marvell. *The Whitsun Weddings*, Faber.

MACCAIG, N. *Riding Lights; The Sinai Sort*, Hogarth. *A Common Grace; A Round of Applause*, Chatto and Hogarth.

NICHOLSON, N. *The Pot Geranium*, Faber.

PLATH, S. *The Colossus and Other Poems*, Heinemann.

PORTER, P. *Once Bitten Twice Bitten;* Poems Ancient and Modern, Scorpion.

SILKIN, J. *The Peaceable Kingdom; The Two Freedoms*, Chatto and Windus.

THOMAS, R. S. *Song at the Year's Turning; Poetry for Supper; Tares*, Hart-Davis.

WAIN, J. *A Word Carved on a Sill*, Routledge; *Weep Before God*, Macmillan.

5. Surveys

The British Council has made four surveys of English verse since 1939 and these have been published by Longmans. Each survey contains an appreciation of individual poets, photographs, and a bibliography. The following surveys have been published:

SPENDER, S.	*Poetry since 1939*	Longmans 1946.
ROSS, A.	*Poetry 1945–1950*	Longmans 1951.
MOORE, G.	*Poetry Today*	Longmans 1958.
JENNINGS, E.	*Poetry Today*	Longmans 1961.

Acknowledgements

We are grateful to the following for permission to reproduce copyright material:

Angus & Robertson Ltd. for 'Gulliver' by Kenneth Slessor from *Poems*; The Belknap Press of Harvard University Press for 'Four Trees upon a Solitary Acre', 'I stepped from plank to plank', and 'After a Hundred Years' by Emily Dickinson from *The Poems of Emily Dickinson* edited by Thomas H. Johnson, Copyright 1951 and 1955 by The President and Fellows of Harvard College; the author's agents for 'In a Bath Teashop' and 'The Planster's Vision' by John Betjeman, published by John Murray Ltd; The Bodley Head Ltd. for 'Mallard' by Rex Warner from *Poems and Contradictions*; Chatto and Windus Ltd. for 'Dulce et Decorum Est' by Wilfred Owen from *The Collected Poems of Wilfred Owen*, and 'A Daisy' by John Silkin; the author's agents for 'The Zebras' by Roy Campbell from *Adamastor*; J. M. Dent & Sons, Ltd. for 'The War Against the Trees' by Stanley Kunitz from *Selected Poems*; the Trustees of the Dylan Thomas Estate and J. M. Dent & Sons, Ltd. for 'The force that through the Green Fuse' by Dylan Thomas from *Collected Poems*; Eyre & Spottiswoode (Publishers) Ltd. for 'Old Woman' by Iain Crichton Smith from *Thistles and Roses*; the author for 'Suicides' by J. C. Hall; Faber & Faber Ltd. for 'Refugee Blues' and 'The Unknown Citizen' from *Collected Shorter Poems*, and 'The Sabbath' from *Homage to Clio* by W. H. Auden, 'November' from *Lupercal*, 'The Jaguar', 'The Martyrdom of Bishop Farrar' and 'Bayonet Charge' from *Hawk in the Rain* by Ted Hughes, 'Sunday Morning' by Louis MacNeice from *Collected Poems*, 'Then' and 'The Horses' by Edwin Muir from *Collected Poems*, 'The Undiscovered Plant' by Norman Nicholson from *The Pot Geranium*, 'Bombing Casualties in Spain' by Herbert Read from *Collected Poems*, and 'The Images of Death' by Michael Roberts from *Collected Poems*; the author's agents for 'The Image' by Roy Fuller; the Trustees of the Estate of Thomas Hardy, Macmillan & Co. Ltd. and The Macmillan Company of Canada Ltd. for

'The Convergence of the Twain', 'Transformations', 'The Last Chrysanthemum', and 'I Look into my Glass' by Thomas Hardy from *The Collected Poems of Thomas Hardy*; George G. Harrap & Co. Ltd. for 'Cloud-Burst' by Geoffrey Johnson from *The Ninth Wave*; Rupert Hart-Davis Ltd. for 'One Furrow' by R. S. Thomas from *Song at the Year's Turning*; The Hogarth Press Ltd. for 'Laggandoan Harris' by Norman MacCaig from *Riding Lights*; Holt, Rinehart & Winston Inc. for 'Design', 'Storm Fear' and 'Our Hold on the Planet' by Robert Frost from *The Complete Poems of Robert Frost*, and 'Happiness' by Carl Sandburg from *Chicago Poems*, both published by Jonathan Cape Ltd.; the author for 'Thistles' by Ted Hughes; Mr. T. Hughes for 'Mushrooms' by Sylvia Plath from *The Colossus and Other Poems*; Hutchinson & Co. (Publishers) Ltd. for 'The Red Balloon' and 'Public Library' by Dannie Abse from *Poems, Golders Green*; the author's agents for 'One Flesh' by Elizabeth Jennings, published by Andre Deutsch Ltd.; the author's agents for 'Field of Autumn' by Laurie Lee from *Bloom of Candles*, published by John Lehmann and Doubleday & Company, Inc.; Mr. John Lehmann for 'Song of the Twentieth Century Man' and 'This Excellent Machine' from *Collected Poems 1930–1963*; Macmillan & Co. Ltd. and The Macmillan Company of Canada Ltd. for 'Au Jardin des Plantes' by John Wain from *Weep Before God*; the Literary Executors of the late Frederic Manning for 'Koré' from *Poems of Frederic Manning*; The Marvell Press for 'Wires' and 'Toads' by Philip Larkin from *The Less Deceived*; Mr. Hubert Nicholson on behalf of the Estate of the late A. S. J. Tessimond for 'The Man in the Bowler Hat' from *Voices in a Giant City*, and 'Black Monday Lovesong' from *Selection* by A. S. J. Tessimond; Oxford University Press for 'Rugby League Game' by James Kirkup from *Refusal to Conform*, and 'Salthouse, Norfolk' by John Press from *Guy Fawkes Night*; Penguin Books Ltd. for lines from 'King Oedipus' by Sophocles from *The Theban Plays*, translated by E. F. Watling; Laurence Pollinger Ltd. and the Estate of the late Mrs. Frieda Lawrence for 'Discord in Childhood' and 'Work' by D. H. Lawrence from *The Complete Poems of D. H. Lawrence*, published by William Heinemann Ltd. and The Viking Press Inc.; Putnam & Co. Ltd. for 'Hospital for Defectives' by Thomas

Blackburn from *The Next Word*, 'Me and the Animals' by David
Holbrook from *Imaginings*, and 'Incendiary' by Vernon Scannell
from *A Sense of Danger*; Random House, Inc. for 'Auto-Wreck'
by Karl Shapiro from *Person, Place and Thing* published by Martin
Secker & Warburg Ltd.; the Editor of *The Royal Air Forces
Quarterly* for 'High Flight' by the Rev. John Gillespie Magee,
first published in that journal in 1941; the author's agents for
'Martha of Bethany' by Clive Sansom from *The Witnesses and
Other Poems* published by Methuen & Co. Ltd.; Scorpion Press
for 'Your Attention Please' by Peter Porter; Martin Secker &
Warburg Ltd. for 'Eli, Eli, Lama Sabachthani?' by W. R.
Rodgers; The Society of Authors for 'Hunger' by Laurence
Binyon, and the author for 'African Beggar' by Raymond
Tong.

We have been unable to trace the copyright owners in 'Drought'
by Denys Lefebvre and would welcome any information that
would enable us to do so.

Index of Poets